A place of dreams, of magic and memories, where fairies grew and spiders spun spells. A place where the wild boy watches. Is he real, or is Elaine lost in her imagination?

Wild Girl, Wild Boy is a gripping and emotionally engaging play by one of today's most innovative and exciting writers. Winner of the Whitbread Children's Book of the Year Award and the Carnegie Medal, David Almond is the author of the critically acclaimed novels *Skellig*, *Kit's Wilderness*, *Heaven Eyes* and *Secret Heart*, and the collection of short stories, *Counting Stars*.

Praise for David Almond:

'A story of love and faith, written with exquisite, heart-fluttering tenderness. It is an extraordinarily profound book, no matter what the age of the reader.' (*Skellig*) THE CHAIRMAN OF THE WHITBREAD JUDGES

'...this superb piece of lyrically-written literary fiction captivates children and their parents alike.' (*Kit's Wilderness*) THE GUARDIAN

'David Almond understands the joy and fear of being alive better than most – *Heaven Eyes* is a mysterious gift of a novel.' THE TIMES

'This gripping book will enrich your soul and fire your imagination.' (*Secret Heart*) THE DAILY TELEGRAPH

'Confirms Almond as a writer of compelling individual vision.' (*Counting Stars*) THE SCOTSMAN

David Almond

Wild Girl Girl Wild Boy

A PLAY

Hodder
Children's
Books

a division of Hodder Headline Limited

PREFACE

This is the tale of Elaine Grew, a brave and troubled young soul. She lives with her mother in an estate on the edge of a northern city. Outside the estate is an open hillside, a group of allotments, a lark-filled sky. Elaine has been happy here, but last year her dad died and now Elaine's in turmoil. She can't think straight, she can't see straight, she can't read or write. She squabbles and fights with her mother, who fears that Elaine is losing her mind, that she's losing touch with the world. Elaine's neighbours and school mates turn away from her. They mock her and scorn her and even fear her. Her teachers don't know what to do with her. Elaine begins to stay away from school. She spends day after day in the wilderness of her dad's old allotment. She crawls like a lizard on the earth as she used to when he was with her. She slithers like a snake through the thorns and weeds. She works spells with spiders and digs in the earth for magic seeds.

What is she searching for? What will she find in the overgrown allotment, this place of memories, dreams and enchantment? And who is this wild boy, who watches her, and begins to move towards her?

For Mike Dalton

Wild Girl, Wild Boy was commissioned by the Lyric Theatre, Hammersmith, and the Pop-Up Theatre Company.

The play was first performed at the Lyric Theatre Hammersmith, London on 10th February 2001 in association with the Pop-Up Theatre Company, directed by Michael Dalton, with the following cast:

JANET BAMFORD	*Elaine*
MARK HUCKETT	*McNamara/Doctor*
ANDREW OLIVER	*Wild Boy/Father*
MANDY VERNON-SMITH	*Mother*

DIRECTOR	Michael Dalton
ASSISTANT DIRECTOR	Jane Wolfson
DESIGNER	Will Hargreaves
MUSIC	Ransom Notes
CO-MUSICAL DIRECTORS	James Hesford
	Mark Pearson
LIGHTING DESIGNER	Ace McCarron
COMPANY STAGE MANAGER	Emma Barron
SET CONSTRUCTION	Set Up Scenery
DIALECT COACH	Majella Hurley

The play received a Sainsbury's Checkout Theatre Award.

CHARACTERS

Elaine Grew, a girl

Elaine's mother

Elaine's father

Mr McNamara, a neighbour

The Wild Boy, also called Skoosh

A doctor

A chorus of voices These are the voices of school mates, teachers, neighbours. These voices provide a cruel commentary that echoes around inside Elaine's head.

SCENE ONE

ELAINE's bedroom. Daytime. Bright blue sky is visible through the window. There is an untidy bed, a table, a chair. She is at a table, trying to write. On the table are pens and pencils, paper and notebooks. There are sheets of drawings, paintings and scribblings scattered on the table and floor. Pictures of birds and animals are pinned to the wall. A shelf on the wall holds pots of paints. Elaine's canvas shoulder bag hangs from her chair.

ELAINE   Wild... Girl... Wild... Boy...
That's the title. Good. That's the title.
Once ... there ... was ... a ... girl ... called ...
Elaine...
Ah. Yes. Phew. That's the start...
She ... lived ... with...

She holds up the paper and looks at her words.

ELAINE   Look at it! Look at it! I'm so stupid. No,
I'm not! I have problems ... writing.
Something to do with the way I ... see
or something.

She looks around, peers into space, as if she's searching for something.

ELAINE   Wild Boy? Wild Boy?
He's gone.
He was here, and now he's gone.

She goes to the window and peers out.

ELAINE   Wild Boy! Where are you? Skooooooosh!
He was here, and now he's gone.

She rattles the window, rattles the door.

ELAINE   Let me out! Let me out!

MUM (*from outside the room*)
Elaine! Elaine, just calm down, love!

ELAINE   Let me out!

MUM   Oh, Elaine. Be a good girl, will you?

ELAINE   Ha, a good girl. That's my mum.
She doesn't understand. She doesn't see.
She's locked me in. Let me out!

Elaine writes again.

ELAINE   She lived with... Agh! Words on me
fingers and on stupid paper slither and
crawl and slip and slide and stagger
like wounded things. Look at them. But
words on me tongue can dance and sing
like larky birds. So I'll tell it to you in
dancing words and show it you in
moving pictures. And I'll tell it to me
rattle as well. This is me rattle I've had
since I was small.

ELAINE takes a big seedhead out of her canvas bag.

ELAINE   A seedhead. A present from me dad.
           Rattle, rattle. Rattle, rattle. You'll wake
           the dead, me mum used to say. You'll
           bring the house down, girl. But she used
           to sing to it as well. And Dad was there
           then, and we were so happy! You should
           have seen the way we went on – specially
           me and Dad. The way we danced! We
           were so happy!

*ELAINE shakes the seedhead. She dances. The sound and
the dance lead her back into the past, into her memories,
into the allotment. At moments like this, her bedroom
and her dad's allotment merge.*
MUM and DAD enter.
DAD comes to ELAINE and joins in with her dance.

MUM   You two! I don't know what I'll do with
           you. You're daft as each other!

*DAD holds some raspberries in his open hands. He holds
out a raspberry towards ELAINE's mouth.*

DAD   Look at this, love. Taste it. It's from deep
           in the heart of the garden, deep in the
           thorns.

ELAINE   It's a raspberry!

ELAINE takes the raspberry, eats it.

DAD   A raspberry. Delicious and wild.
             Oh, watch the juice! Lick it off!

They laugh at the juice and the stains.
DAD holds out a raspberry to MUM.

DAD   Come on. Taste it, love. That's right.

MUM takes a raspberry, eats it.

MUM   So sweet.

DAD   Delicious and sweet and wild. Come on.
             Let yourself go. Let's go wild!

ELAINE   Dance Dad, dance!

They all dance happily, then they stutter to a halt.
They are dejected, exhausted.
DAD exits, leaving MUM and ELAINE alone.
MUM and ELAINE wipe the juice off their faces.
MUM exits.

ELAINE   Then he died, and there was nothing
             more to dance for and nothing more
             to sing for.
             Let me out!
             No answer.

ELAINE is back in the present, alone, in her bedroom.
She puts away her writing things.

ELAINE   Chuck this mess away. This is me.

My name is Elaine. Elaine Grew. This is the story of my Wild Boy. And he's gone, but it's true.

She digs down into her canvas bag. She lifts some pictures from the table.

ELAINE   Look, there's things to show it really happened. Here's the lock of hair I cut when he was fast asleep. Here's the pictures he drew to show the things that he can see and we can't see... That I can't see. In me head's the weird voice, the way he sang.

She sings weirdly.

ELAINE   On me hands is the weird touch of him. In me memory is the weird weird story of him. Keep watching. Keep looking. Keep listening. It starts way back, months back, in a time of doom and gloom and tribulation. Me dad was six months dead. Me lovely dad.

She sings, and shakes the seedhead.

ELAINE   It never woke him.

She shakes the seedhead.

ELAINE   Look. This is what it was like.

*She shakes the seedhead, dances, and she is carried
again into the past.
This time she is in her bedroom, soon after her dad
has died.*

MUM   Elaine! Elaine!

*Mum enters. Elaine rattles her seedhead, sings and
dances wildly.*

MUM   Elaine! How many times do I have to tell
             you?

They struggle over the seedhead.

MUM   You're driving me insane, lass!

ELAINE   Leave me alone! Gerroff me!

Elaine retreats to a corner.

MUM   Look at us. We were so happy.

ELAINE   I was never happy!

MUM   And you were such a lovely girl.

ELAINE   I was never lovely. I've always been
             stupid stupid stupid.

MUM   The school's been on the phone again.
             You've got to go in every day, Elaine, or

we'll be in court before we know it, and what'll that lead to?

ELAINE   School! School! Full of doolies and dipsticks just like me.

MUM   Don't say dooley. You're my lovely girl, Elaine.

ELAINE *rattles the seedhead, dances and sings.*

ELAINE   Rattle rattle! Dooley dipstick thicko dense. Can't read, can't write, can't see straight, can't think straight, can't...

MUM   Oh, Elaine!

ELAINE   Can't ... anything. Rattle rattle. Can't even wake the dead!

MUM   STOP... THAT... NOISE!

MUM *exits.*
ELAINE *shakes the seedhead more slowly.*
We move back into the bedroom in the present.

ELAINE   Aye, we started to fight like that. Fight like cat and dog and cry like babies and run off from each other and hide in corners from each other... So awful.

ELAINE *takes a drawing from the table.*

ELAINE   I'm good at drawing. This is a picture I
              did of me dad. Ages back. I did it in his
              allotment. Laid the paper on a cold frame
              and drew him as he worked. There he is,
              leaning over the earth and the sun
              shining down and the sky so blue and
              the larkybirds singing singing high above.

*She softly shakes the seedhead. It carries her back into
the past, to the allotment.*

DAD enters, whistling softly.
ELAINE leans over her picture, as if drawing it again.
DAD crouches, picks a broken eggshell from the earth.

DAD   Come and see.

ELAINE   What?

DAD   Come and see, love.

ELAINE goes to him.

ELAINE   What is it?

DAD   A lark's egg. See? Speckled white outside.
              And brilliant white inside. A chick came
              out from this. Can you believe it? A little
              chick made from a yellow yolk and a
              salty white that'll one day soon be flying
              over us and singing the loveliest of songs.
              A miracle. Look! Larks, larks, larks.

They stare into the sky, towards the larks.

ELAINE   Can hardly see them, Dad.

DAD   That's right. They fly that high they
nearly disappear. They fly that high you
think they fly right out of the world. But
listen. Listen to their wild sweet song.
There they are.

They listen, and the larks sing.

DAD   That's a lovely picture. How about
putting me name on it, eh?
Go on, it'll be OK. I'll help you.

DAD guides her hand as they form the letters together.

DAD   D... A... D. That's right. Dad. Well done.
Now put your name as the artist.
E... L... A... I... N... E. Elaine. See?
There's you and me both written down.

ELAINE   Dad. Elaine.

DAD   One day soon, we'll have your writing
clear as your drawing, eh? Hey. Let's cut
some of those massive daisies for your
mum. Whoops! Spider.

DAD suddenly plucks something from the air.

DAD   You can work spells with these. Listen.
Spider spider spin your web
Spider spin around my head
Spider spider sit dead still
Spider bring me what I will.
A five-pound note!

DAD flourishes a five-pound note.

DAD   It worked!

ELAINE   Silly!

DAD crouches, as if tending to his plants.
ELAINE softly rattles. She dreams and wonders as her
mind moves between the present and the past.

ELAINE   I've got the picture still. Dad. Elaine.
Dad. Elaine. Looks a mess, but I knew
what it meant...
The allotment. It was a wild place, a
wilderness, and I was his wild girl.
The middle of it was all tame and neat,
but all around: the long grass, the high
weeds, where I crawled and wandered
and got lost and called out to him.

DAD   Go on, little one.

ELAINE   What, Dad?

DAD   Go on. Crawl deep into the wilderness.
Go on. Get lost in there. Go on. I'll be

here. Just call out if you get lost and I'll bring you back to me.

ELAINE crawls and laughs and moves through the wilderness of tall grasses and weeds. She sits up and smiles as she remembers.

ELAINE   The allotment. Place of dreams and magic mixed with leeks and spuds and raspberries ever since I was a little little girl. Crawl crawl I went, like a little lizard, crawl crawl like a little snake. Seeds in me eyes and nose, soil on me hands and knees. Crawling crawling further and further into the wild till me dad called—

DAD   Elaine! Wild girl! Time to come back out!

ELAINE   Yes, Dad!

She shakes the seedhead softly. She dreams and wonders.

ELAINE   Rattle rattle. Rattle rattle. Rattle rattle... There was often someone else there, too. Another man.

McNAMARA enters, stands peering from his own allotment.

ELAINE   McNamara. Had the allotment next to Dad's. Beady eyes, beady stare. Always watching us, he was, always sneering at us. His place was all neat and trim with peas and beans and onions in neat trim rows.

McNAMARA Look at it. Look at the state of it. Like a damn jungle. Hey! What if we all let our gardens go like that, eh?

DAD Eh?

McNAMARA I said, what if we all let our gardens go like that. Get it tidied up, man.

DAD It's tidy enough for us.

McNAMARA Eh? And what about the effect you're having on that poor lass?

DAD There's nothing wrong with her.

McNAMARA Nothing wrong! She'll turn out daft as you are. Poor girl.

ELAINE Usually he said nothing, just watched, just stared. Leaned on his fence and sneered and stared and shook his head and clicked his tongue and stared and stared and stared.

McNAMARA *shakes his head and clicks his tongue and exits.*

DAD I ever show you how to grow a fairy, pet?

ELAINE A fairy, Daddy?

DAD A fairy.

ELAINE   There's no such thing as fairies!

DAD   Yes, there is. But nobody knows you got
           to grow them first, like they was leeks or
           raspberries. A bit of horse muck'll help,
           and a bit of spit.

*DAD plucks a fairy seed from the air. He holds it on
his palm.*

DAD   Look! Here's a fairy seed. Spit on it.

They spit together on the fairy seed.

DAD   Whisper a spell:
           Come along my little fairy, grow like
           mushroom, grow like magic, grow like
           happiness in the heart...

ELAINE   Silly!

DAD   Put it gently on the ground.

*DAD puts the fairy seed on the earth, puts horse muck
and water on it.*

DAD   Then the horse muck. Then the water.
           Then spit again.

They spit again.

DAD   Then just wait.

ELAINE   How long?

DAD   That's the mystery. You can never tell.
Some fairies take ninety-nine years to
grow...

ELAINE   Ninety-nine years!

DAD   And some just take ninety-nine minutes.
Or ninety-nine days. Or ninety-nine
blinks of an eye. Go on, blink ninety-
nine times, keep on wishing, and see if
the fairy grows.

*They blink and count quickly together and end up
in laughter.*

DAD   Not enough. No fairy. Ah, well. Mebbe
this one's a ninety-nine yearer.

ELAINE   Silly!

DAD exits.
ELAINE softly shakes the seedhead.
*She wonders and dreams, and moves between the
present and the past.*

ELAINE   We had fairies planted everywhere in
Dad's allotment. All we ever got of course
was spuds and leeks and raspberries.
Except each night when the fairies
jumped out of the earth and danced like

wind and fire in me dreams. I used to
draw them, draw me dreams.
Fairies!

McNAMARA enters.
ELAINE is drawn back into the past, into the allotment.
He watches her, shakes his head, clicks his tongue.

McNAMARA   Fairies! Ha! Ha! He's leading you astray,
little lady. He doesn't want you to grow
up. He's turning you into a little stupid
wild thing.

ELAINE   No, he's not! No, he's not!

McNAMARA exits.

ELAINE   Was it silly? Was it baby stuff? That's
what Mum said. That's what they all
said. Their voices were all around me.
Their voices echoed through my head.

ELAINE holds her hands around her head as the
voices start.

SCENE TWO

THE CHORUS OF VOICES

(*They are the voices of neighbours, classmates and teachers.*)

– Have you seen the way she just stares out the window with her gob hanging open?

– Like she's catching flies.

– Like a little kid.

– Like a baby.

– And the state of her books?

– Like a spider's crawled over them.

– Like somebody's chucked spaghetti on them.

– Hey, Elaine, has somebody chucked spaghetti on your book?

– No, that's her writing, man!

– Now leave Elaine alone. Oh dear, Elaine. We're going to have to do better than that, aren't we?

– Concentrate, girl!

– Keep your mind on your work.

– Elaine has severe difficulty in maintaining concentration on the task in hand.

– Reading: accuracy?

– Nil.

– Comprehension?

– Nil.

– Reading age?

– Elaine has not yet achieved a score in our current methods of assessment.

– Writing skills?

– Hahahahahahaha!

– She's just out of it, man.

– Round the bend.

– Up the pole.

– Doolally.

– She's upset, man. She's in grief.

– Why's that, then?

– Her dad...

– He was a one, eh?

– Aye, I know, but he died, didn't he?

– Aye.

– Poor soul, eh?

– Aye, poor soul.

– Aye.

– Hey. Listen: Dad's dead and she's losing her head.

– Dad's dead and you're losing your head,
– Dad's dead and you're losing your head,
– Dad's dead and you're...

ELAINE   Stop it! Stop it! Stop it!

MUM comes in, hurries to comfort ELAINE.

MUM   Oh, Elaine, take no notice of them, love.

MUM holds ELAINE tight, then holds her at arm's length.

MUM   But Elaine – you just got to start getting on with it.

ELAINE   I don't know how. I don't know how!

ELAINE and MUM exit.

SCENE THREE

*In the house. MUM is alone. There's a knock on the door.
McNAMARA enters, carrying a tray of beautifully-presented
vegetables, fruits and flowers.*

MUM   Oh, Mr McNamara.

McNAMARA I hope I'm not disturbing you.

MUM   Not at all. Please come in.

McNAMARA I brought you some veg from the
               allotment...

MUM   For us?

McNAMARA ...and some flowers from my garden.

MUM   Oh, you shouldn't have.

McNAMARA I thought I should tell you... I saw Elaine up at the allotment this morning.

ELAINE enters. She recoils when she sees MCNAMARA.

ELAINE What you doing here? What's he doing here?

MUM Calm down, love. It's only Mr McNamara. He's brought some veg for us. Look. Look at this beautiful tomato.

ELAINE It's poison!

MUM Oh, Elaine.

ELAINE He's spit on it. He's put a spell on it. It's poison. Don't touch it! I wouldn't eat it if I was dying of hunger! It's puke! Yuk! You should see his allotment. It's a disgrace! What's he doing here?

MUM Elaine, Mr McNamara says he's seen you out and about when you should be at school. He's seen you in your dad's allotment.

ELAINE Spy! Spy! He's always staring, watching with his evil eye. He thought Dad was stupid and messy and... And he thinks I am as well. Always did, right from when I was a little girl.

MUM   Take no notice, Mr McNamara.

ELAINE   Mum!

MUM   It's because he's worried about you. Because he cares for us!

McNAMARA   I've always been concerned about you, Elaine.

ELAINE   Mum! Can you not see?

MUM   I'm sorry, Mr McNamara.

ELAINE   I'm not! I'm not!

McNAMARA   I understand. It's so difficult. A spirit like hers, and no man in the house...

ELAINE   What? Mum?

MUM   Why don't you leave us, Mr McNamara? I'll calm her down.

McNamara exits. Mum turns angrily to Elaine.

MUM   Now, then, madam...

SCENE FOUR

*ELAINE is in the allotment. She keeps reaching to the
earth, pushing undergrowth aside, searching.*

ELAINE   No fairy. No fairy. No fairy. No fairy.
              Daddy! Daddy! Daddy!

She catches a seed in midair. She spits at it.

ELAINE   Grow like mushroom, grow like magic,
              grow like happiness in the heart.

*She spits at it again, plants it in the earth, puts horse
muck on it.*
She blinks her eyes fast.

ELAINE   Grow like mushroom. Grow like magic.
              Grow like happiness in the heart.
              One two three four five six seven eight...
              Daddy!

McNAMARA enters, watches from his own allotment.
ELAINE looks around, sees him. She catches a spider.

ELAINE   Spider! Big fat spider.
              You can make spells with spiders.
              Spider spider spin your web,
              Spider spin around my head
              Spider spider sit dead still
              Spider work my wicked will.
              Kill McNamara! Ah!

*ELAINE puts the spider down. She turns to MCNAMARA again.
He continues to watch in silence.
ELAINE spits in despair. She sits on the earth. She takes
out paper and pencil from her canvas bag, begins to
draw. She takes out her seedhead. She sings and rattles
to herself, rocks back and forward.
The WILD BOY comes out from the wilderness. He watches
her. He weirdly joins in with her song.*

ELAINE   Oh!

WILD BOY reaches out towards ELAINE.

ELAINE   Don't you dare! Who are you?

*They circle each other. Larks sing high above.
The WILD BOY indicates them with his hands –
a gesture of great tenderness.*

ELAINE   Skylarks. Yes, they're beautiful.

*WILD BOY sings weirdly again – a discordant imitation
of lark song.*

ELAINE   Who are you? Are you wagging it as well?
Which school you at?

WILD BOY discordantly imitates Elaine's voice.

ELAINE   You can't talk! That's all right.
I can't write.
They call me stupid for it, but I'm not.
I'm not!

She reaches out, touches his hands.

ELAINE   Fur. What are you?
                     I can draw, though. Look. I'll draw you.

She draws WILD BOY.

ELAINE   Look. This is you. This is...
                     What's your name?
                     I'll call you... Wild Boy.
                     I can't write it.

She makes a few scribbles to indicate his name.

ELAINE   There. Best I can do. Ha. And here's my
                     name. Elaine. I can just do that.
                     That's who I am. Say my name, Elaine.
                     E-laine.

WILD BOY *weirdly imitates her.*
Suddenly, ELAINE *remembers* MCNAMARA.

ELAINE   Quick! Get back in the weeds where he
                     can't see you.

WILD BOY *doesn't go back.*
MCNAMARA *shakes his head, sighs.*

McNAMARA Silly girl. Stop talking to thin air. Pull
                     yourself together. Get out of there.
                     Get back to school before your mother
                     loses her wits.

He continues to shake his head and to sigh as he watches.

ELAINE   He hasn't seen you. Say my name. E-laine.

WILD BOY   E-ay.

ELAINE   Elaine.

WILD BOY   E-ay.

ELAINE   That's right! That's nearly right!
Oh, Wild Boy! Draw me.
Go on. It's your turn. You draw me.

She pushes the pencil and paper into his hands.
He inspects them, confused.

ELAINE   Just draw what you see.

He moves the pencil across the paper.

ELAINE   Is this what you see? Is this really what
you see? Oh, Wild Boy! Are you a fairy?
Did you grow from the fairy seed I
planted with my dad ninety-nine
weeks ago?

ELAINE gently touches him, inspects him.

ELAINE   No wings. Heavy. Fur on your hands
and feet. You're ... ugly. No, not ugly.
Come with me. Come on. Come on.

ELAINE *tugs his hand. He holds back, glances towards*
MCNAMARA.

ELAINE   Just take no notice of him. He doesn't
            see you, does he? He doesn't see!
            Come on, quick! Come with me.
            Oh, come on, Wild Boy. Let's go home!

*They leave the allotment together. The lark song
intensifies.*
WILD BOY *gazes up to the larks, gestures towards them
again, imitates their song.*
ELAINE *laughs joyfully, tugs at him, and they hurry away.*

SCENE FIVE

THE CHORUS OF VOICES

*The voices commentate on Elaine's return home from
the allotment.*

            – Did you see?

            – Eh?

            – That lass. That Elaine.

– Her again.

– Aye. Did you see her coming down from the allotments?

– Talking to thin air.

– Laughing at thin air.

– Singing at thin air.

– Babbling and laughing like a daft thing, she was.

– Babbling and laughing and pointing at the larks in the sky.

– Too much sun, mebbe.

– It has been blazing hot.

– They put you away for that, you know.

– They don't.

– They do.

– Put you away and chuck away the key.

– They'll come and get her, eh?

– Aye. A big white van and big strong nurses.

– Come on, Elaine, they'll say.

– Come on, love, we'll not harm you.

– This won't hurt a bit.

– Poor soul.

– Aye, poor soul.

– Hee hee hee.

– Wouldn't want her playing with my kids.

– Me neither.

– Not safe, letting her run round like that.

– Shouldn't be allowed.

– Lets the estate down.

– Lock her up, that's what I say.

– Aye. Take her away. Lock her up.

– Lock her up!

SCENE SIX

The kitchen. MUM *is there.*
ELAINE *and* WILD BOY *enter.*

MUM   Where you been, girl? The school's been on again. You've been wagging it again. What am I going to do with you? Oh, Elaine.

ELAINE   I went to the allotment. I found...

MUM   That place again. Why's nobody taken it over yet?
Elaine, all it'll do is make you worse.

ELAINE   I found...

ELAINE *gestures towards* WILD BOY, *showing him to* MUM.
MUM *sees nothing.*

MUM   I talked to the school. I talked to the doctors.

ELAINE   The doctors!

MUM   They want to look at you, Elaine. They want to see...

ELAINE   See what?

MUM   See what's wrong. See if there's anything they can do...

ELAINE holds WILD BOY in front of her mum.
WILD BOY smiles tenderly into MUM'S eyes.
ELAINE realizes that MUM sees nothing.

ELAINE   Look, Mum. Look. Oh, Wild Boy, she
                can't see you. She can't see!

MUM moves close to ELAINE, peers into her eyes.

MUM   Elaine, what's going on in there? What's
                happened to my little girl?

SCENE SEVEN

ELAINE's bedroom. Night. The moon shines in through
the window.
ELAINE is at the table. WILD BOY sits on the table.

ELAINE   Larks soar against the sun by day, bats
                flicker flack against the moon by night.
                You see them, Wild Boy? Flicker flack,
                wild wings in the night.
                Say my name. Elaine. E-laine.

WILD BOY   E-ay.

ELAINE shows him a drawing of the moon, then points at the window and the moon.

ELAINE   That's the moon, Wild Boy. That's the moon that lights the night and pulls the seas and drives us wild. Moooon.

WILD BOY   Oooooo!

ELAINE shakes the seedhead. She starts to dance and yell and sing.
She draws WILD BOY into the dance. He weirdly sings and yells along with her.

ELAINE   Dance, my wild boy. Dance!

MUM (*from outside the room*)
            Elaine! Elaine!

They continue to dance and yell. MUM enters.

MUM   What's going on in here?

ELAINE   Just dancing, Mum.

MUM   You'll bring the house down. You'll...

ELAINE   I'll what.

MUM   You'll drive me wild.

MUM looks around the room. She does not see WILD BOY, but she appears to feel that something is wrong. WILD BOY moves close to her, peers closely at her.

ELAINE   What do you see, Mum?

MUM   What do you mean? Nothing. Your room. What's that...?

ELAINE   That what?

MUM   That ... smell or something. No, not a smell.

MUM moves closer to WILD BOY. She sniffs, narrows her eyes.

ELAINE   Look closer, Mum. Closer.

MUM   What did you do today, at the allotment?

ELAINE   Just mooched. Just dreamed.
Just remembered.

MUM   No fairies?

ELAINE   No fairies.

MUM   I love you. You know that, don't you?

ELAINE   Yes.

MUM   You're such a brave girl.

ELAINE   No, I'm not.

MUM   When the doctors look at you...

ELAINE   They'll see nothing.

MUM   It's because they want to see what they
             can do for you.

ELAINE   They'll do nothing.

MUM   It's because I love you, love.

ELAINE   I know that. Look closely, Mum. Please.
             Look with your ... inside eye.

MUM   Inside eye. Oh, Elaine, what nonsense
             is that?
             I'm looking closely at my lovely girl.

ELAINE   Look closer. See what you can see.

Mum kisses her cheek, hugs her.

MUM   Oh, Elaine. It's so hard for you. Even
             harder than it is for me. But things'll
             get better, my little love. Sleep tight.
             Sweet dreams.

Mum exits.

ELAINE   She doesn't see. She doesn't see you,
              Wild Boy...

SCENE EIGHT

*A Doctor's surgery. On the wall are diagrams of the eye
and the brain, and an eye-test chart.
The* DOCTOR *and* ELAINE *face each other.*
MUM *watches nervously.*
WILD BOY *stands apart, watching, then begins to move
through the room, inspecting it.*

DOCTOR   Look at the letters, Elaine. Tell me which
              ones you can see.

ELAINE   One that's like a tree and one that's like
              a tent and a moon and a half a moon
              and they slither and slide...

MUM   She can't read, Doctor. Not a single word.

DOCTOR   We all have our cross to—

ELAINE   It's not a cross.

DOCTOR   I'd like you to look at these now.

The DOCTOR shows ELAINE a series of cards containing blots and blotches.

DOCTOR   Just say what you see, Elaine. Don't worry. Nobody's trying to catch you out. Just say what you see. Come on, try to take part.

MUM   D'you realize what this is costing, Elaine?

ELAINE   I see a larkybird's heart thumping in the dark. I see the onions run to seed. I see me mum's tongue flapping and flipping when she whispers I was such a lovely girl. I see me dad...

DOCTOR   What?

MUM   Your dad what?

ELAINE   I see him planting fairies in the garden.

DOCTOR   Fairies?

MUM   She's turning back into a baby, Doctor. Her dad was lovely, but some of the things he told her...

ELAINE   Fairies. He's got spit and horse muck on his hands. We count to ninety-nine... Wild Boy! We grew a wild boy, not a fairy!

DOCTOR   A wild boy?

ELAINE   A wild boy!

She looks at WILD BOY *and laughs.*

DOCTOR   What are you looking at now, Elaine?
                What are you seeing now?

The DOCTOR *goes to* ELAINE *with an eye torch in his hand.*
She recoils but he holds her. He shines it into her eye.

DOCTOR   Just stay calm, Elaine. I need to look
                inside, deep inside.

ELAINE   What you looking at? Get off! Get off!

WILD BOY *moves to the* DOCTOR*'s back. He pulls the*
DOCTOR*'s hand away from* ELAINE.
The DOCTOR *is alarmed, amazed, uncomprehending.*
ELAINE *goes to* WILD BOY. *They hold hands and laugh.*
They begin to dance and sing.
The DOCTOR *pulls himself together, takes a notebook*
from his pocket, begins to write as he watches ELAINE*'s*
antics.
She giggles at him, then plucks a spider from the air
before her face.

ELAINE   Spider!
                Spider spider spin your web
                Spider spin into my head
                Spider spider sit dead still
                Spider work my wicked will.
                Doctor, be gone!

She giggles, seeing that nothing happens to the DOCTOR.

ELAINE Ah, well, it doesn't always work. Pretty
      spider.

She runs to the eye-test chart, points to the letters.

ELAINE That's E for Elaine. That's D for Dad.
      That's M for Mum.
      That's W for Wild Boy. See!
      Dance, Wild Boy, dance!

ELAINE dances, yells and sings with WILD BOY.
The DOCTOR gives up writing, goes to MUM.

MUM   Stop it, Elaine! You'll...

ELAINE I know I will. Dance, Wild Boy, dance!
      Dance and yell.
      Yell that hard we'll wake the dead!

ELAINE and WILD BOY run off, leaving the DOCTOR and
MUM disturbed and bemused.

SCENE NINE

*Elaine's bedroom. Night. The moon shines through
the window.*
WILD BOY is on the bed, staring at the moon.
ELAINE crouches with her ear to the floor, listening.

ELAINE   McNamara. He's been here for hours
               downstairs with Mum.

WILD BOY   Oooooo.

ELAINE   That's right. Moon. Mooooon.

WILD BOY   Moooon.

ELAINE   Yes! E-laine.

WILD BOY   E-laine.

ELAINE   Yes! Yes! You can talk! What's your name?

WILD BOY   E-laine.

ELAINE   No. That's my name.

WILD BOY   E-laine?

ELAINE   No. Your name. Never mind. Where did
               you come from? You understand? Where
               did you come from? Draw it!

WILD BOY draws. He now has more control over the pencil. He passes what he has drawn to ELAINE.

ELAINE   That's me, isn't it? But draw me other things.

WILD BOY draws again. As he draws, he looks around him, as if seeing things that ELAINE cannot see.

ELAINE   What are these, Wild Boy? Where do you see these?

WILD BOY points into the spaces around them. He tries to show her what he sees.

ELAINE   Here? Now? I see nothing.

WILD BOY laughs and murmurs, as if communicating with another.
He puts down the paper and pencils and begins to dance, as if with another.
ELAINE watches in fascination and frustration.

ELAINE   Who you dancing with, Wild Boy? Oh, if I could see through your eyes.

McNAMARA *(from outside)*
           Elaine! Elaine Grew!

ELAINE   McNamara!

McNamara comes in, switches the light on.

ELAINE   MUM!

McNAMARA   Your mum will see you later. She told
            me about your performance today in
            the doctor's.

*He picks up the scattered drawings. He paces the room
looking about him.*
Wild Boy follows him closely, watches him closely.

McNAMARA   You have to learn the ways of the world,
            girl.

ELAINE   What are you doing here?

McNAMARA   You have to knuckle down. You have to
            control yourself.

ELAINE   You're nothing to do with me!

McNAMARA   These things, for instance. They're like
            products of a twisted mind.

ELAINE   Spider spider spin your web
            Spider spin around my head...

*Wild Boy moves closer to McNamara, holds his face
close to his.*

McNAMARA   What's that ... smell or something?

ELAINE   Spider spider sit dead still
Spider work my wicked will...

McNAMARA   I saw you, as a little girl, wriggling
through the grass, crawling through the
weed, slithering through the mud.
I heard him, urging you on.

ELAINE   Kill McNamara!

McNAMARA   She'll grow up wrong, I used to say. You
got to train kids proper, just like plants.
You got to stake them and prune them
and shape them. Otherwise... She's
growing up wrong, I used to say. And
after all these years, you've growed up
wrong, Elaine Grew. Growed up wrong,
like a plant gone wild. You need training...

*He crumples the drawings, breaks pencils, takes up
the seedhead and discards it again.*
WILD BOY's *stance becomes more sinister, more threatening.*

McNAMARA   Put away the things of childhood,
Elaine Grew.

ELAINE   Kill McNamara. Kill!

McNAMARA   Crawl back out of the wilderness.

ELAINE   Kill McNamara! Kill!

McNAMARA   Come into the real world. What's that ...
           smell or something?

ELAINE   Spider spider spin your web...

WILD BOY's face is almost touching McNAMARA's.

McNAMARA   What's that ... something. Agh, something!

ELAINE   Spider spin around my head...

McNAMARA   What d'you get up to here, in the
           darkness, on your own?

ELAINE   Spider spider sit dead still...

McNAMARA   One day, maybe soon...

ELAINE   Spider work my wicked will.

McNAMARA   ...I will take your father's part.

ELAINE   Kill McNamara. Kill!

McNAMARA   One day, maybe very soon.

ELAINE   Shut him up!

*WILD BOY clamps his hand across McNAMARA's mouth.
McNAMARA recoils in shock, then retreats slowly.
WILD BOY follows, as if herding McNAMARA out.*

McNAMARA   What do you get up to, in here, in the
            dark, in the light of the moon? What's
            that ... something? Wild girl. Wild girl.
            We'll have to tame you.

McNamara *exits.*
Wild Boy *dances in triumph.*
Elaine *burns with anger.*

ELAINE   Moooooon!

WILD BOY   Ooooooooooo!

SCENE TEN

Elaine's bedroom. Later the same night.
Elaine *and* Wild Boy *crouch on her bed, bathed in*
moonlight.
Elaine *has been cutting paper into the shapes of letters.*
She holds up letters in random patterns.
Wild Boy *watches, as if determined to listen and learn.*

ELAINE   I've made a word out of letters. It's a
              name, your name. Don't know what it
              says, but when I say it I say Skoosh.
              Skoosh!
              Lovely sound, lovely word, lovely name.
              Where do sounds and words and names
              come from? From deep in the deep in
              the deep of your heart.
              Where do letters come from? From a
              table top, from the point of a pen, from
              the pictures running round the walls.
              How do you make the noises from inside
              your heart match up with letters in the
              world?
              I don't know. I'll call you Skoosh.

*She holds the letters before her mouth as she speaks
the word.*
She throws the letters into the air and lets them scatter.
WILD BOY *laughs and plays at catching the letters.*

ELAINE   How does it happen? How do you make
              the letters catch the word? How do you
              make the sound catch the letters? I can't
              do it, but I make the sound. Skoosh. The
              letters don't matter. Skoosh! Skoosh!

MUM *enters. She stands in the doorway, watching.*

ELAINE   What is your name?

WILD BOY   Skoosh.

ELAINE   What is my name?

WILD BOY Elaine.

ELAINE   See? Hear? I taught him how to talk.

MUM   I'm keeping you in, my girl!

ELAINE   Mum!

MUM   I'm at the end of my tether. What can I
                     do? I'm locking you in.

*MUM **exits, closing the door.***
*ELAINE **rushes to the door, finds it locked.***
She rattles the window.

ELAINE   Door locked. Window locked. Let me out!
                     No way out, my Wild Boy Skoosh.

WILD BOY Skoosh.

ELAINE   Hahaha. Skoosh!

WILD BOY Mooooon!

ELAINE   Moooooon!
                     Skoosh! Listen. We'll make a wilderness
                     here in my room. We'll make a garden
                     where we can crawl like lizards, like snakes,
                     where we can slither deep into the wild.

WILD BOY   Wiiiiild!

ELAINE   Yes, Wild Boy. Now, what do we need? Soil, plants, sunlight, rain. Useless.

ELAINE runs to the door and the window, rattles them.

ELAINE   Let me out!

WILD BOY (*trying to imitate Elaine*)
E eee ou! E ee ou!

ELAINE   Shh. No. Listen, Wild Boy Skoosh. My dad... Yes, my dad. You don't know my dad but he was wonderful. My dad said that the greatest of all gardens is the mind. He said in the mind you can grow anything. Anything!

WILD BOY   E-y-ing.

ELAINE   Anything, that's right. We can dream a garden. We can imagine a garden. Dream it, Wild Boy. Close your eyes and watch it grow.

ELAINE closes her eyes, dreams and imagines. WILD BOY copies her, keeps glancing at her to check that he's imagining properly.

ELAINE   You have to see the onions and raspberries and leeks and the flowers,

and you have to feel the soil in your
fingers and under your feet and you
have to feel where the edge of the
wilderness is...

WILD BOY   I-er-ess.

ELAINE   That's right. Wilderness! Can you see it
and feel it, Wild Boy Skoosh? Can you
smell the soil and the scents of the
flowers and feel the sun on you and
the breeze and... Can you see anything,
Skoosh?

*WILD BOY is becoming distracted. He looks away from
ELAINE, towards the moonlight pouring through the
window, towards the outside world.*
*ELAINE opens her eyes, calls to him. But he has grown
lethargic.*

ELAINE   Skoosh!

WILD BOY (*half-heartedly*)
        Skoosh!

ELAINE   Look, this is the earth and these are
raspberries and this is a chrysanthemum
and this is the edge of the... Let me out!

WILD BOY   E ee ou!

ELAINE   Mum!

WILD BOY   U!

ELAINE   Let me out!

MUM (*from outside*)
              Elaine! Elaine, just calm down, love!

ELAINE   Let me out!

MUM (*from outside*)
              Oh, Elaine. Be a good girl, will you?

ELAINE   Let me out! Let me out!

*WILD BOY **clambers on to the bed. He lies there,
dispirited.***
*ELAINE **becomes more desperate, more yearning.***

ELAINE   Oh, isn't it lovely here, Skoosh? The sun,
              the air. Can you hear those lovely lovely
              larkybirds? Look, Wild Boy Skoosh. This
              is the edge of the wilderness – the long
              grass, the high weeds. I'll crawl in there,
              like a little lizard, like a little snake.

*ELAINE **crawls, as if she's in the wilderness of the
allotment, shouldering aside weeds and grasses.***
There is lark song.

ELAINE   Crawl crawl. Seeds in me eyes and nose,
              soil on me hands and knees.
              Oh, look: here's a lark come down!

The song of the lark brings a change.
The bedroom and the allotment merge once more.
WILD BOY exits. DAD enters, whistling softly.

DAD   Go on, little one. Crawl deep into the
wilderness. Go on. Get lost in there. Go
on. I'll be here. Just call out if you get
lost and I'll bring you back to me.

ELAINE   Daddy!

ELAINE doesn't look back.

DAD   Elaine! Elaine! Wild girl! Time to come
back out.

MUM (*from outside*)
        Elaine! Elaine!

DAD exits. MUM comes into the room.

MUM   Elaine! Elaine! What you doing? Elaine.
What you doing on the floor?
Who you been talking to?

ELAINE   Mum. Is he still there?

ELAINE doesn't look back.

MUM   Who? Who?

ELAINE   Oh, Mum, look closely.

MUM   Oh, Elaine, there's nothing. There's
           nobody.

ELAINE   Can you at least see the long grass and
           the raspberries and hear the larkybirds
           singing singing...?

MUM   Oh, my little love.

ELAINE turns and looks.

ELAINE   There's nobody. There's not even Skoosh
           now.

MUM   Oh, Elaine.

ELAINE crouches on the floor, stares into the empty room.

ELAINE   Skoosh! Skoooooooosh!

SCENE ELEVEN

THE CHORUS OF VOICES

– She's crackers, of course.

– Really crackers. Right round the twist.

– Have you heard her? Howling and yowling.

– Chanting and ranting.

– Making a noise fit to wake the dead.

– If you're lucky you'll see her.

– See her?

– Aye. Just watch the window.

– See her dancing like a loony.

– See her banging on the windows.

– Hear her yelling, Let me out!

– Let me out!

– Let me out!

– Her mum must be at the end of her tether, eh?

– Aye. Poor soul.

– Poor soul.

– Thank God she's locked her in.

– Aye. And let's hope she's chucked the
key away.

– Don't want something like that running
round the place.

– Little wild thing howling and yowling.

– Little monster chanting and ranting.

– Little devil doing...

– Just imagine what she could do.

– Such awful things.

– Here! We got kids of our own out here,
you know!

– Keep that wild thing under lock and key!

– We got kids to keep safe out here!

– Just imagine, if she got hold of a child
of yours.

– Aye.

– Aye…

– Just imagine, if *she* was a child of yours.

– No.

– No…

– Don't bear thinking of.

SCENE TWELVE

The Doctor's surgery. ELAINE is dejected, exhausted. She sits opposite the DOCTOR.
MUM stands nervously watching.

DOCTOR   And what did this wild boy look like, Elaine?

MUM   Come on, love. Please join in.

ELAINE	This tall. Arms and legs, just like us. A head, just like us. He was just like us.

ELAINE *looks around the room, as if seeking Wild Boy.*

ELAINE	I keep thinking he'll come back. But I think he went back to the allotment.
DOCTOR	And what else, Elaine? Did he have wings or anything like that?
ELAINE	Wings? Don't be daft.
DOCTOR	A tail, maybe?
ELAINE	Are you joking?
DOCTOR	OK. So what was it that made him ... wild?
ELAINE	He came out of the wilderness...
DOCTOR	The wilderness?
MUM	Her dad's allotment, Doctor. It was always such a mess.
ELAINE	It wasn't a mess. It was beautiful! He couldn't talk... I taught him how to talk. So I can't be that stupid, can I?
MUM	Of course you're not stupid, love.

ELAINE   And he could sing like the larks. And
            there was fur on his hands and feet.

DOCTOR   Fur, Elaine?

ELAINE   Fur. Yes, fur.

DOCTOR   Ah. And ... the kind of fur? Like a cat,
            maybe, or a bear, or...
            What else has fur? Like a fluffy toy, perhaps.

ELAINE   See, you don't believe me. Nobody'll ever
            believe me.

MUM   But, love, you've got to see, it's so...

ELAINE   Dad would have. Dad would have believed.
            Dad would have seen him as well!
            Wild Boy! Skoosh! Where are you?

SCENE THIRTEEN

Elaine's bedroom. Daytime. ELAINE *is crawling on the floor, as if in the allotment.*
MUM *and* McNAMARA *stand watching.*
ELAINE *is absorbed in her own actions and doesn't see them there.*

ELAINE   I'll grow him again. That's what I'll do.
      I'll grow him again.

She catches a fairy seed, spits on it, plants it.

ELAINE   Fairy seed. Horse muck. Spit. In the ground.
      One two three four five six seven...
      No fairy. No Wild Boy.

She crawls again.

ELAINE   Crawl deeper, Elaine. Crawl like a lizard,
      crawl like a snake.

MUM   They said it's grief. They said it's just
      her age. They said to keep an eye on her.
      They said she might just start getting
      better. But they said if she doesn't...

McNAMARA What can I do? Elaine. Elaine!

McNAMARA *moves towards Elaine, but* MUM *holds him back.*
ELAINE *plucks a spider from the earth.*

ELAINE   Spider spider spin your web.

MUM   She gets so lost in her own world.

ELAINE   Spider spin around my head.

MUM   Can't hear, can't see.

ELAINE   Spider spider sit dead still.

McNAMARA Elaine. Elaine!

ELAINE   Spider bring me what I will. Wild Boy. Wild Boy!

MUM   Elaine. Elaine! Where are you?

ELAINE   Horse muck. Spit. Grow like mushroom, grow like magic.
One two three four five...

MUM   Elaine! Elaine!

ELAINE looks up, sees MUM there.

ELAINE   Mum! Fancy seeing you here. Isn't it lovely? Come on in.

MUM   What, love?

ELAINE   Come on in.

MUM   Oh, Elaine!

*MUM looks at MCNAMARA. She wants to join in with
her daughter, but the man's presence inhibits her,
embarrasses her.*

ELAINE   Come on, Mum. Please join in.
                Crawl like a lizard, crawl like a snake.
                Crawl deep into the wilderness.

MUM   Oh, Elaine.

ELAINE   Oh, Mum. It's what Dad would have said.

*MUM sighs, glances at MCNAMARA, then joins ELAINE in
the imaginary allotment.
She crawls beside ELAINE.*

MUM   Where are we, love?

ELAINE   We're at the allotment, Mum. Look, the
                grass, the weeds, the sun shining down,
                the larkybirds singing.

MUM looks around the room.

MUM   We're in your bedroom, love.

ELAINE   Can you not see, can you not hear, can
                you not smell?

MUM   Yes, love.

ELAINE   Good. We might find a fairy in here, you
              know.

MUM   A fairy?

ELAINE   Yes, a real fairy. You can grow them,
              you know.

MUM   Really? Oh, love. Give me a cuddle, love.

MUM *and* ELAINE *hug each other.*

ELAINE   You don't believe me, do you?

MUM   I do.

ELAINE   You can't see anything, can you?

MUM   Yes, I can.

ELAINE   Come with me to the allotment.

MUM   Oh, Elaine.

ELAINE   You've never been, have you, not since...
              You used to come. Do you remember?
              Do you remember how we used to dance
              there, all of us together?

ELAINE tugs her mum's hand. She yearns to leave the
house and take her mother with her, but MUM holds
back, undecided.

McNAMARA   You'll mess her up even worse. You'll
            mess yourself up.

*MUM **looks at him, listens to him, holds** ELAINE.*

McNAMARA   Give her rules and regulations.
            Discipline her. Tame her.
            It's like gardening. How d'you get the
            best plants?
            Proper feeding, proper watering, proper
            pruning. Start growing the wrong way
            and you pull them back.
            Start getting wild and you cut them back.
            You show them what's the right way and
            what's the wrong way to grow. You train
            them, and you keep on training them,
            otherwise there's just ... wilderness.

ELAINE   Come with me, Mum.

*MUM **smiles, turns away from** McNAMARA, **and hurries
off with** ELAINE.*
*McNAMARA **shakes his head, sighs, slowly follows.***

SCENE FOURTEEN

THE CHORUS OF VOICES

They commentate on the journey out of the estate.

– Did you see them?

– Who?

– Daft Elaine Grew and her mother, man.

– The crazy one?

– Aye. Did you see them walking out the estate? Running up the hill to the allotments?

– Weirdos, eh?

– The kid pulling her mum. That bloke McNamara following them.

– They looked wild, eh?

– Wild. Wild.

– The mother looked as crackers as the kid, eh?

– It happens like that with families. One of them starts cracking up and before you know it they're all belting round the twist.

– Climbing up the pole.

– Poor souls.

– Aye. Hee hee hee. Poor souls.

– Mebbe they were chasing fairies.

– Or running after things that weren't there.

– Hey, Elaine, bring us a fairy back!

– Did you hear, though?

– Eh?

– Did you hear the birds?

– The birds?

– Aye. Did you hear the way they were
  singing?

– Now you mention it...

– Never heard them that loud.

– And never seen that many.

– Like the sky was filled with larkybirds
  way up high.

– And the sun that bright and everything
  that still.

– Weird.

– Aye. Weird.

SCENE FIFTEEN

The allotment. MUM *and* ELAINE *enter.*
MUM *looks around her in wonder, touches the earth,*
the plants, smells the air, feels the sun on her face,
listens to the larks that sing high above.
Her whole body relaxes.
She smiles with ELAINE, *and joyful memories move*
through her.
ELAINE *laughs and draws her* MUM *into the weeds*
and long grasses. Her MUM *joins in.*

ELAINE   That's right, Mum. Seeds in your eyes
          and nose, soil on your hands and knees.
          Crawl in deeper, deeper. Come on. We
          might find a fairy in here, you know.

MUM   Might we? A real fairy?

ELAINE   A real fairy.

MUM   Oh, love.

ELAINE   Come on, Mum.
            You can grow them, you know, like they
            was leeks or raspberries.
            Dad showed me... Yes, Dad.
            Look, here's a fairy seed!

ELAINE plucks a fairy seed from the air.

ELAINE   Spit and horse muck.

*She spits on the seed, plants it, throws horse muck
on to it.*

ELAINE   Then the spell:
            Come along, my little fairy, grow like
            mushroom...
            Come on, Mum. Join in. Say it along
            with me.

MUM is shy at first, but then joins in more confidently.

MUM/ELAINE (*together*)
            Grow like mushroom, grow like magic,
            grow like happiness in the heart.

ELAINE   Come on, Mum.

MUM/ELAINE
Grow like mushroom, grow like magic,
grow like happiness in the heart.

ELAINE   Now spit on it again.

MUM   Elaine!

MUM giggles and recoils.

ELAINE   Go on. Spit on it.

MUM spits half-heartedly.

ELAINE   Properly!

MUM   I can't!

ELAINE   Yes, you can.

ELAINE demonstrates how to spit properly.
MUM copies her, laughing.

ELAINE   Now blink dead fast ninety-nine times.

MUM blinks fast.

MUM   Like this?

ELAINE   Yes, like this.

*They blink and count and laugh together and end
in giggles. Then they gaze down at the fairy seed.*

ELAINE   Ah, well. Mebbe this one's a ninety-nine
                yearer.

MUM   A ninety-nine yearer!

ELAINE   Isn't it lovely here, Mum?

MUM   Yes...
                Remember how we used to dance here?

ELAINE   Yes.

MUM   Give us a cuddle, love.

The larks sing. MUM and ELAINE hug each other.
WILD BOY emerges from the wilderness. He watches them.
MUM sees him over ELAINE's shoulder.

MUM   Oh!

ELAINE   Mum?

ELAINE turns and sees WILD BOY.

ELAINE   Didn't I tell you? Oh, Wild Boy, I thought
                you'd gone.

MUM   Wild Boy.

WILD BOY   I oy.

WILD BOY moves towards them.
MUM reaches out and touches his hands.

MUM   Fur! What are you?

ELAINE   It's my Wild Boy, Mum. It's Skoosh.
             What's my name?

WILD BOY   E-laine.

ELAINE   What's your name?

WILD BOY   Skoosh!

MUM   What's my name?

WILD BOY regards her with great tenderness.

MUM   What's my name?

WILD BOY   M-um.

ELAINE   Oh, Wild Boy!

MUM, ELAINE and WILD BOY begin to dance.

ELAINE   Come on, Mum. Come on, Wild Boy.
             Let's wake the dead!

They dance and sing, then become still.
ELAINE reaches down into the grass, picks up an eggshell.

ELAINE   Here's a lark's egg, Mum.
              See, speckled white outside, brilliant
              white inside. A little lark grew out of
              this. From yellow yolk and salty white
              and flew away. A miracle.

MUM   A miracle. You were once a yolky little
              salty thing.
              And look at you now, so lovely.

*MUM and ELAINE are absorbed by their memories and
by the miracle of the eggshell.*
WILD BOY exits.
*DAD enters, whistling softly. He stands watching his
wife and daughter.*
Lark song.

ELAINE   Oh! Here's a lark come down.

MUM and ELAINE are very still. They do not turn.

DAD   Go on. Go on.
              Crawl deep into the wilderness.
              Just call out if you get lost.
              Grow like mushroom, grow like magic,
              grow like happiness in the heart.
              Spider, spider, spin your web.
              Wild girls. Wild girls!

DAD watches.
MUM and ELAINE remain very still. The larks sing.

ELAINE   I love you, Mum.

MUM   I love you.

DAD *exits.*
MCNAMARA *enters, carrying raspberries in his hands.*
MUM *turns.*

MUM   Mr McNamara.

MCNAMARA *is confused, uncertain.*

McNAMARA   The larks are so loud today.

MUM   Were you watching us?

McNAMARA   I tried. I couldn't see. You were in the
             wilderness.
             I saw...

MUM   What?

ELAINE   What?

McNAMARA   The larks so loud. The sun so bright ...
             I brought you these.

MUM   Raspberries.

McNAMARA   They were hanging over my allotment.
             I reached deep into the thorns.

ELAINE   Dad's.

McNAMARA   Yes, your dad's. They're ... delicious.
Sweeter than any I ever grew.

*MUM takes the raspberries from him. She hands one
to ELAINE.*
McNAMARA exits.
MUM and ELAINE eat the raspberries.

MUM   Delicious.

ELAINE   Raspberries. Delicious and sweet and
wild.

They laugh at the juice and the stains.
*WILD BOY comes out from the wilderness. He moves
around them, but they are so absorbed in each other
and in their memories that they do not see him at first.
Then they smile together, seeing that he is there.
He gestures for them to explore the allotment and its
wilderness.*

ELAINE   Come on, Mum.

ELAINE and MUM move into the wilderness.
WILD BOY dances, then follows them.

(END)

AFTERWORD

We lived in a small estate on a steep hill in a small Tyneside town. The centre was just below us: the square with trees and benches, the Co-op, The Blue Bell, The Jubilee. There was a lovely clutter of buildings and names: *Dragone's Cafe*; MAYS' FASHION'S; Howes Junk; SPEED THE PLOUGH TAVERN; Le Palais de Dans. Churches and working men's clubs, busy streets, long queues at bus stops, a steep high street of pork shops and bakers and fishmongers leading down to our railway station. Then were the warehouses and factories, then much further down was the Tyne, and then Newcastle, packed densely on the opposite bank.

Higher up, above our estate, came emptiness, space and light. I remember bright breezy days, leaving the house, leaving the estate, crossing Rectory Road, walking upwards to the playing fields, then the heather hills at the summit of the town. There was a freedom in walking away from the centre, in climbing closer to the massive lark-filled sky.

The allotments were just before the playing fields, squeezed into the space between the houses of Fleming Gardens and Windy Ridge. My grand-father's was the third one up, behind the pointed timber fence. You put your hand through the timbers to unlatch the gate, then stepped on to the cinder path that led past the leek trenches, the chrysanthemums and the cold frames to the greenhouse.

Usually he was waiting there, sitting on a seat of old bricks, gazing out across the fields, puffing on his pipe.

'Aye,' he'd say, turning to acknowledge me, wiping his hand across the grin that had flickered on his face. 'Aye, aye.' And he'd spit, wipe his grin again and turn his face to the fields again.

He was a man with little small talk, with no apparent desire to teach me anything with words. No matter what the season, he wore a dark serge suit, a tightly-fastened waistcoat, white shirt, dark tie, checked cloth cap, and black Oxford boots.

We shared long easy silences, long hours of doing nothing very much. We pottered in the breathless greenhouse and the breezy garden. We lit smouldering smoky fires of weeds. He held me up as I plunged a watering can into the great rainwater butt and watched the great glug and gush and suck the water made around my hand. We watered leeks and onions. We clipped chrysanthemums and plucked sweet warm tomatoes and wrapped them in *Daily Mirrors*. We swigged from huge bottles of lemonade. He lifted his cap, wiped the sweat from his head, replaced the cap again. He tugged at his tight collar. He puffed on his pipe. He spat from one side of his mouth while holding the pipe clenched in the other. He grinned wryly at me. He said, 'Aye' and 'Aye, aye.' He took his watch from his waistcoat pocket and raised his eyes and shook his head at the passing of the day.

If we went back to that time now and leaned on the allotment fence and watched the old man and the boy in there, it might all seem pretty pleasant, pretty aimless, pretty pointless. In some obscure way, though, the boy in there was preparing to be a writer.

Years later I was approached by Sally Goldsworthy, Head of Education at the Lyric Theatre Hammersmith. Would I be interested in writing a play to be included in the theatre's remarkable programme of work for children? I pondered the idea. I sat at my desk before a computer beneath a reading lamp. I contemplated an empty space, a stage, and the memories and sensations of the allotment rushed to fill it.

The smells of turned earth and pipe smoke, onions and leeks and chrysanthemums; the taste of tomatoes and peas and raspberries; the feeling of rough cinders under my feet; the voices of other gardeners, of children yelling far off on the fields. I remembered the factory sirens that wailed at lunchtime, the smell of frying chips from the houses on Windy Ridge. I remembered digging in the dirt with a spoon as an infant, with a spade as a growing boy. I remembered sweat and dirt, blisters on my palms, the sting of sunburn on my neck. I remembered worms and centipedes and beetles, the feeling of them as they moved across an open hand. I remembered the pigeons that wheeled in close fast flocks over our heads, racing back to the pigeon lofts higher up the hill. Over everything, when I recalled that garden and those days, I heard from high above the endless lovely singing of the larks.

Budding writers often ask for advice. What books must be read? What writing practice must be done? Well, there are libraries full of books to be read and reams of notepaper to be filled, and there are great joys and great benefits to be found in the process. But writing isn't a skill like, say, tennis is – a skill that can be strengthened and refined by constant rehearsal of particular moves, constant development of particular muscles. If you do nothing but write in preparation for writing you'll become a very dismal writer. Listening to larks while digging with a spoon in the dirt might look like a kid just mucking about, but in the long run it can be as valuable as a couple of hours extra homework with pen in hand or fingers on the keyboard.

There are other, darker forces at work in *Wild Girl, Wild Boy*, of course. My father died when I was young and when my sisters were much younger. So Elaine's pain is something that I know about. But her story is one of life, not death. She's a bold creative spirit, brave enough to yell and scream at death, brave enough to outface it, brave enough to keep returning to her wilderness and to discover – or create – the means to transcend her pain. This is what the writer does: explore the gardens of the mind, crawl through wilderness, emerge with scratched skin and muddied knees accompanied by words and creatures and images that begin to form themselves into the stories that help to keep the world alive.

Printed stories usually take the form of prose: blocks of print that start at the top left-hand corner of a page, march line by line down to the bottom right, then jump up to the top left again. They're the product of solitary days and weeks and months of scribbling in notebooks, tapping at the keyboard, staring out of the window, hissing in frustration, dreaming, pondering, scribbling again, tapping again, slowly slowly trying to sort a wild tangle of words and notions into a coherent story. In the end, all those lovely lines of print and all those lovely pages look beautifully organized, beautifully controlled.

When I was a boy, and beginning to dream of becoming an author, printed pages were both an inspiration and a hindrance to me. I found them beautiful and I wanted to produce them, but at the same time their beauty intimidated me – they seemed so fixed, so untouchable, the writer who produced them must have such an organized mind. How could I, whose mind seemed a jumble, dare to think that I could do the same?

The fixity of a book, and the static beauty of a printed page, are illusions. A printed story is just a story caught between covers at a particular time.

Caught earlier or later, the story would have a different form. And the untouchable beauty of the page is the work of the typesetter, printer, publisher.

Any good story, no matter how controlled it appears on the page, is not a tame trapped thing. It still has wildness in it, a yearning to break free of its neat lines and numbered pages. And it does break free. It leaps from the page, and moves far beyond the control of the author, as soon as a reader begins to read it.

Reading is a creative, imaginative act. The reader helps to create the book. Each reader creates a different book. Each reader hears different voices, sees different faces and landscapes. Their reading of the book is infected by their own experiences, expectations, dreams and desires. A story is a living thing that escapes from the page and races and prowls through our imaginations.

A play can have even fewer claims to fixity. I began to write *Wild Girl, Wild Boy* as I would a piece of prose – alone in my study in Newcastle. I imagined the empty space, the stage. I began to write Elaine's words. I had a notion of what Elaine looked like, how she sounded, what her room looked like, what her estate looked like, what her mum and dad looked like, how they sounded... They walked and talked and danced in the stage-like space I'd cleared in my mind.

But unlike stories in prose that march line by line from top left to bottom right, all the space filled in by the writer, a story in play form moves down the page in short bursts surrounded by lots of space. Dialogue, names, skimpy stage directions, and that's all. The space around the words is for the director, the actors and the designer to fill.

Pretty soon I was out of my study with a half-finished script and on the train to London to see what would happen to this story when it started to break free.

We workshopped the script in an empty space in Islington; Pop-Up Theatre's director, Mike Dalton; assistant director, Jane Wolfson; four actors; and myself. As soon as the lines were spoken, they became something new – at once very like and very unlike the way I'd heard them in my mind. And each time they were re-spoken, they changed again. I saw what happened in silence in a reader's mind happening in a stage-like space before me.

The story was taking on a new life, was being recreated. It had begun to break away and to prowl through the imaginations of everybody there. Elaine leapt to life, became a real girl in front of me, no longer a notion on a page and in my mind, but a dancing, crawling, singing, yelling character of flesh and blood born not just from my words but from the skills of an actor.

Rewriting was an active and immediate act. If a character's words fell flat we tried out other variations of the words. The half-finished script was soon filled with scribbled notes: my own responses, the responses of the directors and the actors.

We had particular discussions about the character McNamara. In the early draft he was a one-dimensional cardboard cut out: simply sinister, nothing more. I was amazed when an actor showed me how his lines could be spoken to suggest a greater complexity, that there was potential to turn McNamara into a slightly more sympathetic (and believable) character. McNamara remains a sinister force, of course, but I hope I learned to suggest that there might be some true concern and tenderness in him.

I watched and listened and scribbled and discussed and learned. I took my script home, scribbled, pondered, contemplated the stage-space in my mind, reworked, wrote on. I maintained an ongoing e-mail correspondence with Mike Dalton in which we shared our suggestions, our excitements, our doubts. Like a good editor commenting on a story in prose, he was able to pinpoint where a tiny adjustment in particular places would benefit the story overall.

We workshopped again. There were difficulties with pacing, with the sequencing of events. There were clumsy moments. How could we make the chorus of voices work on stage? How could we make the shifts from present to past convincing? I scribbled again, wrote again, the story developed again.

By the time we reached rehearsals, we had the first movements of James Hesford's and Mark Pearson's amazingly atmospheric and evocative music. We had the first mock-up of Will Hargreaves' set: a magical thing that could blend Elaine's bedroom with her dad's allotment with a doctor's surgery, that could evoke the movements of Elaine's restless, yearning mind. We also had a cast: Janet Bamford, Mark Huckett, Andrew Oliver, Mandy Vernon-Smith. Here they were, the people who would finally lift the story from my pages and pass it over to an audience. These actors stepped into the story, danced in it, sang in it, laughed and cried in it, made it their own world. The story was recreated yet again.

By now, the script was just about done: only a few adjustments remained, to make the words flow more easily and rhythmically on the tongue and on the air. More and more, I became an observer. Moment by moment, the story moved further away from me.

I left it there, in the rehearsal space in Islington, and went home again to Newcastle to work on other projects. For *Wild Girl, Wild Boy*, as far as I was concerned, all that remained were a couple of e-mail messages, a couple of phone calls with Mike. While I sat at my desk, the music and the set were completed, the play moved from the space in Islington into a week's rehearsal in its first venue, The Lyric Studio.

I travelled nervously to the first performance. I trembled a little as I went into the theatre. An hour before the performance, I opened the door into the dark studio, stepped inside. A last-minute rehearsal was under way. The music played. Beneath the stage lights were the bedroom, the allotment. The moon shone through the window above the bed. Who was that figure that shuffled through the lights, with his wild hair, his ragged clothes, with fur on his hands and feet? Who was that girl, her face transfigured by a weird mixture of despair and delight?

I only paused there for a few astonished seconds, but in those seconds I looked into a world that I'd helped to create, but that no longer needed me. I stepped back through the door, into the everyday light, and waited with the rest of the audience for the first performance to begin.

In the weeks and months that followed, the play travelled across the country. It appeared in theatres, arts centres, school halls. While I got on with my life in Newcastle, Skoosh came out from the wilderness in Manchester, Elaine wept and yelled in Stirling, McNamara announced his theories on child-raising in Aberystwyth, Dad planted fairies in Hemel Hempstead, Mum nibbled raspberries in Brighton. The set was erected, taken down, erected again, the cast travelled hundreds of miles, the music was played and replayed, the stage-spaces were illuminated and then returned to darkness. The audiences came and watched and went home again. The story ran its course and ran its course again until the tour was over.

In the end, of course, none of it exists. There is no Elaine, there is no Wild Boy, there is no allotment, there is no bedroom. The play is a subterfuge, a set of disguises and tricks. It's a pack of lies. The story of Elaine and Skoosh exists in the minds of those that see the story on the stage, and of those that read their story on the page.

Like all stories, it's a pack of lies that tries to reach out to us and allow us to experience some kind of human truth. Of course it depends on the creative skills of writer, directors, actors, composers, designers. But it also depends on the creative skills of the audience, those skills of the imagination that allow all of us to leap into other minds and other worlds, skills that are at once quite natural, straightforward, commonplace and quite quite amazing.

D. A.